Discover the irresistible softness of t-shirt yarn for home décor projects. The whole family will love these innovative crochet designs ranging from organizers to lounging comforts. The easy patterns and bulky yarns give fast results.

LEISURE ARTS, INC. • Maumelle, Arkansas

HEXAGON MOTIF RUG

EASY

Finished Measurement:

27½" x 28½" (70 cm x 72.5 cm)

SHOPPING LIST

Yarn (Super Bulky Weight) SUPER BULKY 6

[8 ounces, 149 yards
(227 grams, 136 meters) per skein]:

- ☐ White - 1 skein
- ☐ Black - 1 skein
- ☐ Pink - 1 skein

Crochet Hook

- ☐ Size M/N (9 mm)
  or size needed for gauge

Additional Supplies

- ☐ Yarn needle

GAUGE INFORMATION

One Hexagon = 9½" (24.25 cm) from side to side

Gauge Swatch: 4½" (11.5 cm) from side to side

Work same as Hexagon, page 4, through Rnd 2: 24 dc and 6 ch-2 sps.

HEXAGON

(Make 2 White, 3 Black, and 3 Pink)

Rnd 1 (Right side)**:** Ch 4, dc in fourth ch from hook **(3 skipped chs count as first dc, now and throughout)**, ch 2, (2 dc in same st, ch 2) 5 times; join with slip st to first dc: 12 dc and 6 ch-2 sps.

Note: Loop a short piece of yarn around any stitch to mark Rnd 1 as **right** side.

Rnd 2: Ch 3 **(counts as first dc, now and throughout)**, dc in next dc, (dc, ch 2, dc) in next ch-2 sp, ★ dc in next 2 dc, (dc, ch 2, dc) in next ch-2 sp; repeat from ★ 4 times **more**; join with slip st to first dc: 24 dc and 6 ch-2 sps.

Rnd 3: Ch 3, dc in next 2 dc, (dc, ch 2, dc) in next ch-2 sp, ★ dc in next 4 dc, (dc, ch 2, dc) in next ch-2 sp; repeat from ★ 4 times **more**, dc in last dc; join with slip st to first dc: 36 dc and 6 ch-2 sps.

Rnd 4: Ch 3, dc in next 3 dc, (dc, ch 2, dc) in next ch-2 sp, ★ dc in next 6 dc, (dc, ch 2, dc) in next ch-2 sp; repeat from ★ 4 times **more**, dc in last 2 dc; join with slip st to first dc: 48 dc and 6 ch-2 sps.

Rnd 5: Ch 3, dc in next 4 dc, (dc, ch 2, dc) in next ch-2 sp, ★ dc in next 8 dc, (dc, ch 2, dc) in next ch-2 sp; repeat from ★ 4 times **more**, dc in last 3 dc; join with slip st to first dc, finish off: 60 dc and 6 ch-2 sps.

HALF HEXAGON (Make 2)

Row 1: With White, ch 4, dc in fourth ch from hook, (ch 2, 2 dc in same st) twice; do **not** join: 6 dc and 2 ch-2 sps.

Row 2 (Right side)**:** Ch 3, turn; dc in first 2 dc, (dc, ch 2, dc) in next ch-2 sp, dc in next 2 dc, (dc, ch 2, dc) in next ch-2 sp, dc in next dc, 2 dc in last dc: 12 dc and 2 ch-2 sps.

Note: Mark Row 2 as **right** side.

Rows 3-5: Ch 3, turn; dc in first dc, ★ dc in next dc and in each dc across to next ch-2 sp, (dc, ch 2, dc) in ch-2 sp; repeat from ★ once **more**, dc in each dc across to last dc, 2 dc in last dc: 30 dc and 2 ch-2 sps.

Finish off.

Using Placement Diagram as a guide and working through inside loops only, whipstitch Hexagons together to form 2 strips of 3 Hexagons **each** ***(Fig. 3b, page 31)***, beginning in second ch of one corner ch-2 and ending in first ch of next corner ch-2. Whipstitch remaining 2 Hexagons and 2 Half Hexagons together in same manner to form center strip; then whipstitch strips together.

PLACEMENT DIAGRAM

COASTER & PLACEMAT SET

EASY

Finished Measurements: **Coaster** - 4" (10 cm) square **Placemat** - 12" x 18" (30.5 cm x 45.5 cm)

SHOPPING LIST

Yarn (Bulky Weight) [5 BULKY]

[8.8 ounces, 317 yards (250 grams, 290 meters) per skein]:

- ☐ 1 skein will make 1 coaster and 1 placemat **or** 2 placemats

Crochet Hooks

- ☐ **Coaster:** Size J (6 mm)
- ☐ **Placemat:** Size K (6.5 mm) **or** sizes needed for gauge

GAUGE INFORMATION

With larger size hook,
10 dc = 4" (10 cm), 6 rows = 3¾" (9.5 cm)

Gauge Swatch: 4" wide x 3¾" high (10 cm x 9.5 cm)

With larger size hook, ch 12.

Row 1: Dc in fourth ch from hook **(3 skipped chs count as first dc)** and in each ch across: 10 dc.

Rows 2-6: Ch 3 **(counts as first dc)**, turn; dc in next dc and in each dc across.

Finish off.

STITCH GUIDE

TREBLE CROCHET ***(abbreviated tr)***
YO twice, insert hook in st indicated, YO and pull up a loop (4 loops on hook), (YO and draw through 2 loops on hook) 3 times.

COASTER

With smaller size hook, ch 13.

Row 1: Dc in fourth ch from hook **(3 skipped chs count as first dc)** and in each ch across: 11 dc.

Row 2: Ch 3 **(counts as first dc, now and throughout)**, turn; dc in next dc, ch 3, skip next 2 dc, tr in next 3 dc, ch 3, skip next 2 dc, dc in last 2 dc.

Rows 3-5: Ch 3, turn; dc in next dc, ch 3, skip next ch-3 sp, sc in next 3 sts, ch 3, skip next ch-3 sp, dc in last 2 dc.

Row 6: Ch 3, turn; dc in next dc, ch 3, skip next ch-3 sp, tr in next 3 sc, ch 3, skip next ch-3 sp, dc in last 2 dc.

Row 7: Ch 3, turn; dc in next dc, 2 dc in next ch-3 sp, dc in next 3 tr, 2 dc in next ch-3 sp, dc in last 2 dc; finish off.

PLACEMAT

With larger size hook, ch 31.

Row 1: Dc in fourth ch from hook **(3 skipped chs count as first dc)** and in each ch across: 29 dc.

Row 2: Ch 3 **(counts as first dc, now and throughout)**, turn; dc in next dc and in each dc across.

Row 3: Ch 3, turn; dc in next dc, ★ ch 3, skip next 2 dc, tr in next 3 dc, ch 3, skip next 2 dc, dc in next 2 dc; repeat from ★ across.

Rows 4-6: Ch 3, turn; dc in next dc, ★ ch 3, skip next ch-3 sp, sc in next 3 sts, ch 3, skip next ch-3 sp, dc in next 2 dc; repeat from ★ across.

Row 7: Ch 3, turn; dc in next dc, ★ ch 3, skip next ch-3 sp, tr in next 3 sc, ch 3, skip next ch-3 sp, dc in next 2 dc; repeat from ★ across.

Row 8: Ch 3, turn; dc in next dc, ★ 2 dc in next ch-3 sp, dc in next 3 tr, 2 dc in next ch-3 sp, dc in next 2 dc; repeat from ★ across: 29 dc.

Rows 9-28: Ch 3, turn; dc in next dc and in each dc across.

Edging (Right side)**:** Ch 1, turn; 3 sc in first dc, sc in each dc across to last dc, 3 sc in last dc; sc evenly across end of rows; working in free loops of beginning ch ***(Fig. 2, page 31)***, 3 sc in first ch, sc in next 27 chs, 3 sc in next ch; sc evenly across end of rows; join with slip st to first sc, finish off.

LAUREN CONRAD celebrate

OVAL RUG

EASY

Finished Measurement:

Approximately 23" x 40" (58.5 cm x 101.5 cm)

SHOPPING LIST

Yarn (Bulky Weight)

[8.8 ounces, 317 yards

(250 grams, 290 meters) per skein]:

- ☐ Grey - 1 skein
- ☐ Variegated - 1 skein

Crochet Hook

- ☐ Size M/N (9 mm)
  or size needed for gauge

GAUGE INFORMATION

9 sts = 4" (10 cm)

Gauge Swatch: 1¾" wide x 18½" long (4.5 cm x 47 cm)

Work same as Rug, page 10, through Rnd 2: 86 sc.

STITCH GUIDE

TREBLE CROCHET ***(abbreviated tr)***

YO twice, insert hook in dc indicated, YO and pull up a loop (4 loops on hook), (YO and draw through 2 loops on hook) 3 times.

RUG

With Variegated, ch 39.

Rnd 1 (Right side)**:** Sc in second ch from hook and in each ch across to last ch, 3 sc in last ch; working in free loops of beginning ch ***(Fig. 2, page 31)***, sc in next 37 chs, 3 sc in next unworked ch; join with slip st to first sc: 80 sc.

Note: Loop a short piece of yarn around any stitch to mark Rnd 1 as **right** side.

Rnd 2: Ch 1, sc in same st as joining and in each sc across to next 3-sc group, place marker after sc just made to indicate beginning of shaping, 2 sc in each of next 3 sc, sc in each sc across to last 3 sc, place marker, 2 sc in each of last 3 sc; join with slip st to first sc: 86 sc.

Rnd 3: Ch 1, sc in same st as joining, ★ sc in each sc across to marker, move marker up, (sc in next sc, 2 sc in next sc) 3 times; repeat from ★ once **more**; join with slip st to first sc: 92 sc.

Continue to move markers up.

Rnd 4: Ch 1, sc in same st as joining, ★ sc in each sc across to marker, 2 sc in next sc, (sc in next 2 sc, 2 sc in next sc) twice; repeat from ★ once **more**, sc in last 2 sc; join with slip st to first sc: 98 sc.

Rnd 5: Ch 1, sc in same st as joining, ★ sc in each sc across to marker, (sc in next 3 sc, 2 sc in next sc) 3 times; repeat from ★ once **more**; join with slip st to first sc, finish off: 104 sc.

Rnd 6: With **right** side facing, join Grey with dc in same st as joining ***(see Joining With Dc, page 31)***; ★ dc in next sc and in each sc across to marker, (dc in next 4 sc, 2 dc in next sc) 3 times; repeat from ★ once **more**; join with slip st to first dc, finish off: 110 dc.

Rnd 7: With **right** side facing, join Variegated with sc in same st as joining ***(see Joining With Sc, page 31)***; ★ sc in each dc across to marker, (sc in next 5 dc, 2 sc in next dc) 3 times; repeat from ★ once **more**; join with slip st to first sc: 116 sc.

Rnd 8: Ch 1, sc in same st as joining, ★ sc in each sc across to marker, 2 sc in next sc, (sc in next 6 sc, 2 sc in next sc) twice; repeat from ★ once **more**, sc in last 6 sc; join with slip st to first sc: 122 sc.

Rnd 9: Ch 1, sc in same st as joining, ★ sc in each sc across to marker, (sc in next 7 sc, 2 sc in next sc) 3 times; repeat from ★ once **more**; join with slip st to first sc, finish off: 128 sc.

Rnd 10: With **right** side facing, join Grey with dc in same st as joining; ★ dc in next sc and in each sc across to marker, (dc in next 8 sc, 2 dc in next sc) 3 times; repeat from ★ once **more**; join with slip st to first dc, finish off: 134 dc.

Rnd 11: With **right** side facing, join Variegated with sc in same st as joining; ★ sc in each dc across to marker, (sc in next 9 dc, 2 sc in next dc) 3 times; repeat from ★ once **more**; join with slip st to first sc: 140 sc.

Rnd 12: Ch 1, sc in same st as joining, ★ sc in each sc across to marker, 2 sc in next sc, (sc in next 10 sc, 2 sc in next sc) twice; repeat from ★ once **more**, sc in last 10 sc; join with slip st to first sc: 146 sc.

Rnd 13: Ch 1, sc in same st as joining, ★ sc in each sc across to marker, (sc in next 11 sc, 2 sc in next sc) 3 times; repeat from ★ once **more**; join with slip st to first sc, finish off: 152 sc.

Rnd 14: With **right** side facing, join Grey with dc in same st as joining; ★ dc in next sc and in each sc across to marker, (dc in next 12 sc, 2 dc in next sc) 3 times; repeat from ★ once **more**; join with slip st to first dc, finish off: 158 dc.

Rnd 15: With **right** side facing, join Variegated with sc in same st as joining; ★ sc in each dc across to marker, (sc in next 13 dc, 2 sc in next dc) 3 times; repeat from ★ once **more**; join with slip st to first sc: 164 sc.

Rnd 16: Ch 1, sc in same st as joining, ★ sc in each sc across to marker, 2 sc in next sc, (sc in next 14 sc, 2 sc in next sc) twice; repeat from ★ once **more**, sc in last 14 sc; join with slip st to first sc: 170 sc.

Rnd 17: Ch 1, sc in same st as joining, ★ sc in each sc across to marker, (sc in next 15 sc, 2 sc in next sc) 3 times; repeat from ★ once **more**; join with slip st to first sc, finish off: 176 sc.

Rnd 18: With **right** side facing, join Grey with dc in same st as joining; ★ dc in next sc and in each sc across to marker, (dc in next 16 sc, 2 dc in next sc) 3 times; repeat from ★ once **more**; join with slip st to first dc, finish off: 182 dc.

Rnd 19: With **right** side facing, join Variegated with sc in same st as joining; ★ sc in each dc across to marker, (sc in next 17 dc, 2 sc in next dc) 3 times; repeat from ★ once **more**; join with slip st to first sc: 188 sc.

Rnd 20: Ch 1, sc in same st as joining, ★ sc in each sc across to marker, 2 sc in next sc, (sc in next 18 sc, 2 sc in next sc) twice; repeat from ★ once **more**, sc in last 18 sc; join with slip st to first sc: 194 sc.

Rnd 21: Ch 1, sc in same st as joining, ★ sc in each sc across to marker, (sc in next 19 sc, 2 sc in next sc) 3 times; repeat from ★ once **more**; join with slip st to first sc, finish off: 200 sc.

Rnd 22: With **right** side facing, join Grey with dc in same st as joining; ★ dc in next sc and in each sc across to marker, remove marker, (dc in next 20 sc, 2 dc in next sc) twice; repeat from ★ once **more**, dc in last 21 sc; join with slip st to first dc: 204 dc.

Rnd 23: Ch 4 **(counts as first dc plus ch 1)**, skip next dc, (dc in next dc, ch 1, skip next dc) around; join with slip st to first dc: 102 dc.

Rnd 24: Ch 5 **(counts as first tr plus ch 1)**, tr in same st as joining, (ch 1, tr in same st) 3 times, skip next dc, ★ tr in next dc, (ch 1, tr in same st) 4 times, skip next dc; repeat from ★ around; join with slip st to first tr, finish off.

LAUREN CONRAD celebrate
SERÉ PRINCE HALVERSON
The Underside of Joy
JK ROWLING
FANTASTIC BEASTS
THE ORIGINAL SCREENPLAY
LEAH HAGER COHEN

BASKET SET

●●○○ EASY

Finished Measurements:

Large - 32" (81.5 cm) circumference

Medium - 25½" (65 cm) circumference

Small - 19¼" (49 cm) circumference

SHOPPING LIST

Yarn (Bulky Weight) BULKY 5

[8.8 ounces, 317 yards
(250 grams, 290 meters) per skein**]**:

- ☐ Cream - 1 skein
- ☐ Variegated - 1 skein

Crochet Hook

- ☐ Size K (6.5 mm)
  or size needed for gauge

GAUGE INFORMATION

10 sc = 4" (10 cm)

Gauge Swatch: 2" (5 cm) diameter
Work same as Bottom of any Basket, page 14, through Rnd 2: 16 sc.

LARGE BASKET

BOTTOM

Rnd 1 (Right side)**:** With Variegated, ch 2, 8 sc in second ch from hook; do **not** join, place marker to indicate beginning of rnd ***(see Markers, page 30)***.

Note: Loop a short piece of yarn around any stitch to mark Rnd 1 as **right** side.

Rnd 2: 2 Sc in each sc around: 16 sc.

Rnd 3: (Sc in next sc, 2 sc in next sc) around: 24 sc.

Rnd 4: (Sc in next 2 sc, 2 sc in next sc) around: 32 sc.

Rnd 5: (Sc in next 3 sc, 2 sc in next sc) around: 40 sc.

Rnd 6: (Sc in next 4 sc, 2 sc in next sc) around: 48 sc.

Rnd 7: (Sc in next 5 sc, 2 sc in next sc) around: 56 sc.

Rnd 8: (Sc in next 6 sc, 2 sc in next sc) around: 64 sc.

Rnd 9: (Sc in next 7 sc, 2 sc in next sc) around: 72 sc.

Rnd 10: (Sc in next 8 sc, 2 sc in next sc) around; remove marker, slip st in next sc, do **not** finish off: 80 sc.

SIDES

Rnd 1: Ch 1, sc in Back Loop Only of each st around ***(Fig. 1, page 31)***; join with slip st to first sc.

Rnd 2: Ch 1, sc in both loops of each sc around; do **not** join, place marker.

Rnds 3-14: Sc in each sc around.

Slip st in next sc, finish off.

CUFF

Rnd 1: With **right** side facing, join Cream with sc in same st as slip st ***(see Joining With Sc, page 31)***; sc in each sc around; join with slip st to first sc.

Rnd 2: Ch 1, **turn**; sc in each sc around; do **not** join, place marker.

Rnds 3-10: Sc in each sc around.

Slip st in next sc, finish off.

Fold Cuff to right side.

MEDIUM BASKET

BOTTOM

Rnds 1-8: Work same as Large Basket: 64 sc.

Slip st in next sc, remove marker.

SIDES

Rnds 1-12: Work same as Large Basket.

Slip st in next sc, finish off.

CUFF

Work same as Large Basket.

SMALL BASKET

BOTTOM

Rnds 1-6: With Cream, work same as Large Basket: 48 sc.

Slip st in next sc, remove marker.

SIDES

Rnds 1-12: Work same as Large Basket.

Slip st in next sc, finish off.

CUFF

Rnds 1-10: With Variegated, work same as Large Basket.

Slip st in next sc, finish off.

Fold Cuff to right side.

TEXTURED PILLOW

●●○○ EASY

Finished Measurement: 16" (40.5 cm) square

SHOPPING LIST

Yarn (Bulky Weight) BULKY 5

[8.8 ounces, 317 yards (250 grams, 290 meters) per skein]:

- ☐ 1 skein

Crochet Hook

- ☐ Size M/N (9 mm) **or** size needed for gauge

Additional Supplies

- ☐ Yarn needle
- ☐ Pillow form - 16" (40.5 cm) square

GAUGE INFORMATION

In pattern,

10 sts = 4¼" (10.75 cm),6 rows = 3½" (9 cm)

Gauge Swatch: 4¼" wide x 3½" high (10.75 cm x 9 cm)

Ch 12.

Work same as Back, page 17, for 6 rows: 10 sts.

Finish off.

STITCH GUIDE

CLUSTER (uses one sc)

★ YO twice, insert hook in sc indicated, YO and pull up a loop, (YO and draw through 2 loops on hook) twice; repeat from ★ 4 times **more**, YO and draw through all 6 loops on hook.

FRONT

Ch 38.

Row 1: Dc in fourth ch from hook **(3 skipped chs count as first dc, now and throughout)** and in each ch across: 36 dc.

Row 2: Ch 1, turn; sc in each st across: 36 sc.

Row 3 (Right side)**:** Ch 3 **(counts as first dc, now and throughout)**, turn; dc in next 3 sc, work Cluster in next sc, (dc in next 2 sc, work Cluster in next sc) across to last 4 sc, dc in last 4 sc: 10 Clusters and 26 dc.

Row 4: Ch 1, turn; sc in each st across: 36 sc.

Row 5: Ch 3, turn; dc in next 5 sc, work Cluster in next sc, (dc in next 2 sc, work Cluster in next sc) across to last 5 sc, dc in last 5 sc: 9 Clusters and 27 dc.

Rows 6-8: Repeat Rows 2-4.

Row 9: Ch 3, turn; dc in next sc and in each sc across.

Row 10: Ch 1, turn; sc in each dc across.

Rows 11-18: Repeat Rows 9 and 10, 4 times.

Rows 19-25: Repeat Rows 3-9.

Edging: Ch 1, do **not** turn; work 34 sc evenly spaced across end of rows; working in free loops of beginning ch ***(Fig. 2w, page 31)***, 3 sc in first ch, sc in next 34 chs, 3 sc in next ch; work 34 sc evenly spaced across end of rows; 3 sc in first dc, sc in each dc across to last dc, 3 sc in last dc; join with slip st to first sc, finish off: 148 sc.

BACK

Ch 38.

Row 1 (Right side)**:** Dc in fourth ch from hook and in each ch across: 36 dc.

Note: Loop a short piece of yarn around any stitch to mark Row 1 as **right** side.

Row 2: Ch 1, turn; sc in each dc across.

Row 3: Ch 3, turn; dc in next sc and in each sc across.

Rows 4-25: Repeat Rows 2 and 3, 11 times.

Edging: Work same as Front.

Whipstitch Front and Back together matching beginning chs and inserting pillow form before closing ***(Fig. 3a, page 31)***.

STRIPED BASKET

●●○○ EASY

Finished Measurement:

31" circumference x 7" high (78.5 cm x 18 cm)

SHOPPING LIST

Yarn (Super Bulky Weight) SUPER BULKY 6

[8 ounces, 149 yards

(227 grams, 136 meters) per skein]:

- ☐ Grey - 1 skein
- ☐ White - 1 skein
- ☐ Purple - 1 skein

Crochet Hook

- ☐ Size M/N (9 mm)
  or size needed for gauge

GAUGE INFORMATION

9 sts = 4" (10 cm)

Gauge Swatch: 3" (7.5 cm) diameter

Work same as Bottom through Rnd 2: 20 sc.

BOTTOM

Rnd 1 (Right side)**:** With Grey, ch 4, 9 dc in fourth ch from hook **(3 skipped chs count as first dc)**; join with slip st to first dc: 10 dc.

Note: Loop a short piece of yarn around any stitch to mark Rnd 1 as **right** side.

Rnd 2: Ch 1, 2 sc in each dc around; join with slip st to first sc: 20 sc.

Rnd 3: Ch 3 **(counts as first dc, now and throughout)**, 2 dc in next sc, (dc in next sc, 2 dc in next sc) around; join with slip st to first dc: 30 dc.

Rnd 4: Ch 1, sc in same st as joining and in next dc, 2 sc in next dc, (sc in next 2 dc, 2 sc in next dc) around; join with slip st to first sc: 40 sc.

Rnd 5: Ch 3, dc in next 2 sc, 2 dc in next sc, (dc in next 3 sc, 2 dc in next sc) around; join with slip st to first dc: 50 dc.

Rnd 6: Ch 1, sc in same st as joining and in next 3 dc, 2 sc in next dc, (sc in next 4 dc, 2 sc in next dc) around; join with slip st to first sc: 60 sc.

Rnd 7: Ch 3, dc in next 4 sc, 2 dc in next sc, (dc in next 5 sc, 2 dc in next sc) around; join with slip st to first dc, do **not** finish off: 70 dc.

SIDES

Rnd 1: Ch 1, hdc in Back Loop Only of each dc around ***(Fig. 1, page 31)***; join with slip st to first hdc.

Rnds 2 and 3: Ch 1, hdc in both loops of each hdc around; join with slip st to first hdc.

Finish off.

Rnd 4: With **right** side facing and working in both loops, join White with hdc in same st as joining (***see Joining With Hdc, page 31)***; hdc in next hdc and in each hdc around; join with slip st to first hdc, finish off.

Rnd 5: With **right** side facing and working in Back Loops Only, join Purple with hdc in same st as joining; hdc in next hdc and in each hdc around; join with slip st to first hdc, finish off.

Rnd 6: With Grey, repeat Rnd 5.

Rnds 7-12: Repeat Rnds 4-6 twice; do **not** finish off at end of Rnd 12.

Rnd 13: Ch 1, working in both loops, hdc in same st as joining and in next 12 hdc, ch 12 (handle), skip next 10 hdc, hdc in next 25 hdc, ch 12, skip next 10 hdc, hdc in last 12 hdc; join with slip st to first hdc: 50 hdc and 24 chs.

Rnd 14: Ch 1, hdc in same st as joining and in next 12 hdc, 12 hdc in next ch-12 sp, hdc in next 25 hdc, 12 hdc in next ch-12 sp, hdc in last 12 hdc; join with slip st to first hdc, finish off.

TOTE

●●○○ EASY

Finished Measurement:

26½" circumference x 11" high

(67.5 cm x 28 cm)

SHOPPING LIST

Yarn (Bulky Weight) BULKY 5

[8.8 ounces, 317 yards

(250 grams, 290 meters) per skein**]**:

- ☐ Cream - 1 skein
- ☐ Black - 1 skein

Crochet Hook

- ☐ Size I (5.5 mm)

  or size needed for gauge

Additional Supplies

- ☐ Purse handles with rings

GAUGE INFORMATION

12 sts = 4" (10 cm)

Gauge Swatch: 4" (10 cm) wide

With Black, ch 13.

Row 1: Sc in second ch from hook and in each ch across: 12 sc.

Rows 2-6: Ch 1, turn; sc in each sc across.

Finish off.

STITCH GUIDE

DOUBLE CROCHET 2 TOGETHER

(abbreviated dc2tog)

(uses next 2 dc)

★ YO, insert hook in **next** dc, YO and pull up a loop, YO and draw through 2 loops on hook; repeat from ★ once **more**, YO and draw through all 3 loops on hook **(counts as one dc)**.

BOTTOM

With Black, ch 31.

Row 1: Sc in second ch from hook and in each across: 30 sc.

Rows 2-10: Ch 1, turn; sc in each sc across.

SIDES

Rnd 1 (Right side)**:** Ch 1, do **not** turn; sc in end of each row across; sc in free loop of each ch across ***(Fig. 2, page 31)***; sc in end of each row across; sc in each sc across; join with slip st to first sc: 80 sc.

Note: Loop a short piece of yarn around any stitch to mark Rnd 1 as **right** side.

Rnds 2-10: Ch 1, sc in Back Loop Only of each sc around ***(Fig. 1, page 31)***; join with slip st to first sc.

Finish off.

Rnd 11: With **right** side facing and working in Back Loops Only, join Cream with dc in same st as joining ***(see Joining With Dc, page 31)***; dc in next sc and in each sc around; join with slip st to first dc.

Rnd 12: Ch 3, dc **around** ch-3 just made, skip next dc, ★ dc in both loops of next dc, dc **around** post of dc just made, skip next dc; repeat from ★ around; join with slip st to top of beginning ch.

Rnd 13: Ch 3 **(counts as first dc, now and throughout)**, dc in next dc and in each dc around; join with slip st to first dc.

Rnds 14-20: Repeat Rnds 12 and 13, 3 times; then repeat Rnd 12 once **more**.

Rnd 21: Ch 3, dc in next 10 dc, dc2tog, (dc in next dc, dc2tog) 9 times, dc in next 11 dc, dc2tog, (dc in next dc, dc2tog) 9 times; join with slip st to first dc: 60 dc.

Rnd 22: Ch 1, sc in each dc around; join with slip st to first sc.

Flatten Tote; using photo as a guide, mark placement for ends of both handles.

Rnd 23: Ch 1, ★ sc in each sc across to sc before marker, holding ring in **front** of work and working around ring, sc in next 3 sc; repeat from ★ 3 times **more**, sc in each sc across; join with slip st to first sc, finish off.

LARGE POUF

●●○○ EASY

Finished Measurement:

Approximately 18" diameter x 56" circumference x 9" high (45.5 cm x 142 cm x 23 cm)

SHOPPING LIST

Yarn (Super Bulky Weight) SUPER BULKY 6

[8 ounces, 149 yards

(227 grams, 136 meters) per skein]:

- ☐ Blue - 2 skeins
- ☐ Grey - 2 skeins

Crochet Hook

- ☐ Size M/N (9 mm)

  or size needed for gauge

Additional Supplies

- ☐ Yarn needle
- ☐ Polyester fiberfill

GAUGE INFORMATION

8 Linked dc = 4" (10 cm),

3 rows = 2¾" (7 cm)

Gauge Swatch: 3½" (9 cm) diameter

Work same as Top, page 24, through Rnd 3: 24 sc.

STITCH GUIDE

BEGINNING LINKED DOUBLE CROCHET

(abbreviated beginning Linked dc)

Pull up a loop in second ch from hook and in same st as slip st (3 loops on hook), (YO and draw through 2 loops on hook) twice.

LINKED DOUBLE CROCHET

(abbreviated Linked dc)

Pull up a loop in horizontal bar of st just made ***(Fig. A)*** and in next st ***(Fig. B)*** (3 loops on hook), (YO and draw through 2 loops on hook) twice.

Fig. A

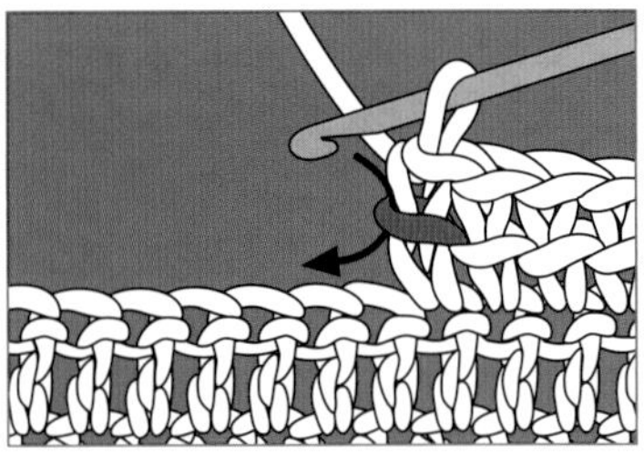

Fig. B

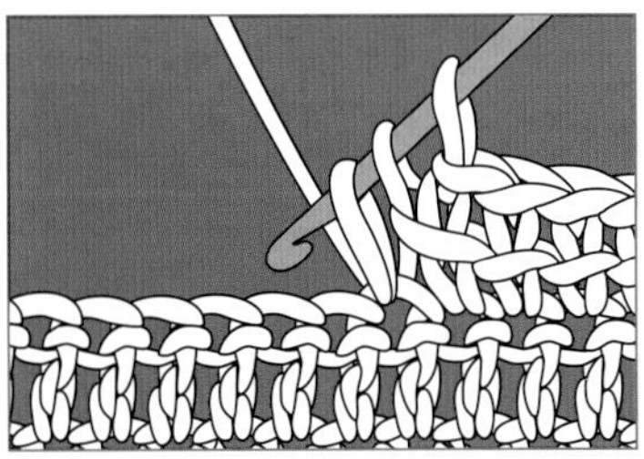

TOP

Rnd 1 (Right side)**:** With Blue, ch 2, 8 sc in second ch from hook; do **not** join, place marker to indicate beginning of rnd ***(see Markers, page 30)***.

Note: Loop a short piece of yarn around any stitch to mark Rnd 1 as **right** side.

Rnd 2: 2 Sc in each sc around: 16 sc.

Rnd 3: (2 Sc in next sc, sc in next sc) around: 24 sc.

Rnd 4: (Sc in next 2 sc, 2 sc in next sc) around: 32 sc.

Rnd 5: (2 Sc in next sc, sc in next 3 sc) around: 40 sc.

Rnd 6: (Sc in next 4 sc, 2 sc in next sc) around: 48 sc.

Rnd 7: (2 Sc in next sc, sc in next 5 sc) around: 56 sc.

Rnd 8: (Sc in next 6 sc, 2 sc in next sc) around: 64 sc.

Rnd 9: (2 Sc in next sc, sc in next 7 sc) around: 72 sc.

Rnd 10: 2 Sc in next sc, sc in next 15 sc, (2 sc in next sc, sc in next 13 sc) around: 77 sc.

Rnd 11: (2 Sc in next sc, sc in next 10 sc) around: 84 sc.

Rnd 12: (Sc in next 11 sc, 2 sc in next sc) around: 91 sc.

Rnd 13: (2 Sc in next sc, sc in next 12 sc) around: 98 sc.

Rnd 14: (Sc in next 48 sc, 2 sc in next sc) twice: 100 sc.

Rnd 15: (Sc in next 24 sc, 2 sc in next sc) around: 104 sc.

Rnd 16: (2 Sc in next sc, sc in next 25 sc) around: 108 sc.

Rnd 17: (Sc in next 26 sc, 2 sc in next sc) around; slip st in next sc, finish off: 112 sc.

BOTTOM

Work same as Top.

SIDE

Rnd 1: With **right** side of Top facing and working in Back Loops Only ***(Fig. 1, page 31)***, join Grey with slip st in last slip st made; ch 3, work beginning Linked dc, work Linked dc around; join with slip st to beginning Linked dc.

Rnds 2-10: Ch 3, working in Back Loops Only, work beginning Linked dc, work Linked dc around; join with slip st to beginning Linked dc.

Finish off.

Whipstitch Bottom to Side ***(Fig. 3b, page 31)***, working through inside loops only and stuffing Pouf with polyester fiberfill before closing.

DOILY RUG

●●○○ **EASY**

Finished Measurement: Approximately 30" (76 cm) diameter

SHOPPING LIST

Yarn (Bulky Weight)

[8.8 ounces, 317 yards
(250 grams, 290 meters) per skein]:

- ☐ 2 skeins

Crochet Hook

- ☐ Size M/N (9 mm) **or** size needed for gauge

GAUGE INFORMATION

Gauge Swatch: 4½" (11.5 cm) diameter
Work same as Rug through Rnd 2: 24 dc and 12 ch-1 sps.

STITCH GUIDE

TREBLE CROCHET *(abbreviated tr)*
YO twice, insert hook in st or sp indicated, YO and pull up a loop (4 loops on hook), (YO and draw through 2 loops on hook) 3 times.

BEGINNING CLUSTER
(uses one st or sp)
★ YO twice, insert hook in st or sp indicated, YO and pull up a loop, (YO and draw through 2 loops on hook) twice; repeat from ★ 3 times **more**, YO and draw through all 5 loops on hook.

CLUSTER (uses one st or sp)
★ YO twice, insert hook in st or sp indicated, YO and pull up a loop, (YO and draw through 2 loops on hook) twice; repeat from ★ 4 times **more**, YO and draw through all 6 loops on hook.

RUG

Ch 5; join with slip st to form a ring.

Rnd 1 (Right side)**:** Ch 5 **(counts as first dc plus ch 2)**, (dc in ring, ch 2) 11 times; join with slip st to first dc: 12 dc and 12 ch-2 sps.

Rnd 2: Slip st in first ch-2 sp, ch 3 **(counts as first dc)**, dc in same sp, ch 1, (2 dc in next ch-2 sp, ch 1) around; join with slip st to first dc: 24 dc and 12 ch-1 sps.

Rnd 3: Slip st in next dc and in next ch-1 sp, ch 3, work beginning Cluster in same sp, ch 4, (work Cluster in next ch-1 sp, ch 4) around; join with slip st to top of beginning Cluster: 12 Clusters and 12 ch-4 sps.

Rnd 4: ★ (2 Sc, dc, ch 1, dc, 2 sc) in next ch-4 sp, slip st in next Cluster; repeat from ★ around working last slip st in joining slip st.

Rnd 5: Ch 3 (**counts as first dc**), skip next 3 sts, slip st in next ch-1 sp, skip next 3 sts, ★ 5 dc in next slip st, skip next 3 sts, slip st in next ch-1 sp, skip next 3 sts; repeat from ★ around, 4 dc in same st as first dc; join with slip st to first dc: 72 sts.

Rnd 6: Ch 1, (2 sc in next slip st, sc in next 5 dc) around; join with slip st to first sc: 84 sc.

Rnd 7: Slip st in next sc, ch 4 (**counts as first tr**), 2 tr in same st, ch 1, skip next 2 sc, 2 tr in next sc, ★ ch 1, skip next 3 sc, 3 tr in next sc, ch 1, skip next 2 sc, 2 tr in next sc; repeat from ★ around to last 2 sc, skip last 2 sc; sc in first tr to form last ch-1 sp: 60 tr and 24 ch-1 sps.

Rnd 8: Ch 4 (**counts as first tr**), 2 tr in last ch-1 sp made, 3 tr in each ch-1 sp around; join with slip st to first tr: 72 tr.

Rnd 9: Slip st in next tr, ch 3, work beginning Cluster in same st, ch 4, skip next 2 tr, ★ work Cluster in next tr, ch 4, skip next 2 sts; repeat from ★ around; join with slip st to top of beginning Cluster: 24 Clusters and 24 ch-4 sps.

Rnds 10-14: Repeat Rnds 4-8: 144 tr.

Rnd 15: Ch 4 (**counts as first dc plus ch 1**), (dc in next tr, ch 1) around; join with slip st to first dc.

Rnd 16: Ch 1, sc in each dc and in each ch-1 sp around; join with slip st to first sc, finish off.

THROW

●●○○ EASY

Finished Measurement:

39¼" x 41" (99.5 cm x 104 cm)

SHOPPING LIST

Yarn (Bulky Weight) BULKY 5

[8.8 ounces, 317 yards

(250 grams, 290 meters) per skein]:

- ☐ 4 skeins

Crochet Hook

- ☐ Size M/N (9 mm)
  or size needed for gauge

GAUGE INFORMATION

In pattern,12 sts = 4½" (11.5 cm),

6 rows = 3" (7.5 cm)

Gauge Swatch: 5¾" wide x 4½" high (14.5 cm x 11.5 cm)

Ch 17.

Row 1: Dc in fourth ch from hook **(3 skipped chs count as first dc)** and in each ch across: 15 dc.

Row 2: Ch 1, turn; sc in first 3 dc, (ch 3, skip next 3 dc, sc in next 3 dc) across.

Row 3: Ch 1, turn; sc in first 3 sts, (ch 3, skip next 3 chs, sc in next 3 sts) across.

Row 4: Ch 3, turn; dc in next 2 sc, (ch 3, skip next 3 chs, dc in next 3 sc) across.

Rows 5 and 6: Repeat Row 3 twice.

Rows 7-9: Repeat Rows 4-6.

Finish off.

THROW

Ch 107.

Row 1: Dc in fourth ch from hook **(3 skipped chs count as first dc)** and in each ch across: 105 dc.

Rows 2 and 3: Ch 3 **(counts as first dc, now and throughout)**, turn; dc in next dc and in each dc across.

Row 4: Ch 3, turn; dc in next 2 dc, (ch 3, skip next 3 dc, dc in next 3 dc) across: 17 ch-3 sps and 54 dc.

Rows 5 and 6: Ch 1, turn; sc in first 3 sts, (ch 3, skip next 3 chs, sc in next 3 sts) across.

Row 7: Ch 3, turn; dc in next 2 sc, (ch 3, skip next 3 chs, dc in next 3 sc) across.

Repeat Rows 5-7 for pattern until Throw measures approximately 39½" (100.5 cm) from beginning ch, ending by working Row 7.

Next Row: Ch 3, turn; dc in next 2 dc, (3 dc in next ch-3 sp, dc in next 3 dc) across: 105 dc.

Last 2 Rows: Ch 3, turn; dc in next dc and in each dc across.

Finish off.

GENERAL INSTRUCTIONS

ABBREVIATIONS

ch(s)	chain(s)
cm	centimeters
dc	double crochet(s)
dc2tog	double crochet 2 together
hdc	half double crochet(s)
mm	millimeters
Rnd(s)	Round(s)
sc	single crochet(s)
sp(s)	space(s)
st(s)	stitch(es)
tr	treble crochet(s)
YO	yarn over

SYMBOLS & TERMS

★ — work instructions following ★ as many **more** times as indicated in addition to the first time.

( ) or **[ ]** — work enclosed instructions **as many** times as specified by the number immediately following **or** work all enclosed instructions in the stitch or space indicated **or** contains explanatory remarks.

colon (:) — the number(s) given after a colon at the end of a row or round denote(s) the number of stitches or spaces you should have on that row or round.

GAUGE

Exact gauge is **essential** for proper size. Before beginning your project, make the sample swatch given in the individual instructions in the yarn and hook specified. After completing the swatch, measure it, counting your stitches and rows carefully. If your swatch is larger or smaller than specified, **make another, changing hook size to get the correct gauge**. Keep trying until you find the size hook that will give you the specified gauge.

MARKERS

Markers are used to help distinguish the beginning of each round being worked. Place a 2" (5 cm) scrap piece of yarn before the first stitch of each round, moving marker after each round is complete.

CROCHET TERMINOLOGY		
UNITED STATES		INTERNATIONAL
slip stitch (slip st)	=	single crochet (sc)
single crochet (sc)	=	double crochet (dc)
half double crochet (hdc)	=	half treble crochet (htr)
double crochet (dc)	=	treble crochet (tr)
treble crochet (tr)	=	double treble crochet (dtr)
double treble crochet (dtr)	=	triple treble crochet (ttr)
triple treble crochet (tr tr)	=	quadruple treble crochet (qtr)
skip	=	miss

Yarn Weight Symbol & Names	LACE 0	SUPER FINE 1	FINE 2	LIGHT 3	MEDIUM 4	BULKY 5	SUPER BULKY 6	JUMBO 7
Type of Yarns in Category	Fingering, size 10 crochet thread	Sock, Fingering, Baby	Sport, Baby	DK, Light Worsted	Worsted, Afghan, Aran	Chunky, Craft, Rug	Super Bulky, Roving	Jumbo, Roving
Crochet Gauge* Ranges in Single Crochet to 4" (10 cm)	32-42 sts**	21-32 sts	16-20 sts	12-17 sts	11-14 sts	8-11 sts	6-9 sts	5 sts and fewer
Advised Hook Size Range	Steel*** 6 to 8, Regular hook B-1	B-1 to E-4	E-4 to 7	7 to I-9	I-9 to K-10½	K-10½ to M/N-13	M/N-13 to Q	Q and larger

*GUIDELINES ONLY: The chart above reflects the most commonly used gauges and hook sizes for specific yarn categories.

** Lace weight yarns are usually crocheted with larger hooks to create lacy openwork patterns. Accordingly, a gauge range is difficult to determine. Always follow the gauge stated in your pattern.

*** Steel crochet hooks are sized differently from regular hooks–the higher the number, the smaller the hook, which is the reverse of regular hook sizing.

JOINING WITH SC

When instructed to join with sc, begin with a slip knot on hook. Insert hook in stitch or space indicated, YO and pull up a loop, YO and draw through both loops on hook.

JOINING WITH HDC

When instructed to join with hdc, begin with a slip knot on hook. YO, holding loop on hook, insert hook in stitch or space indicated, YO and pull up a loop, YO and draw through all 3 loops on hook.

JOINING WITH DC

When instructed to join with dc, begin with a slip knot on hook. YO, holding loop on hook, insert hook in stitch or space indicated, YO and pull up a loop (3 loops on hook), (YO and draw through 2 loops on hook) twice.

BACK LOOP ONLY

Work only in loop(s) indicated by arrow ***(Fig. 1)***.

Fig. 1

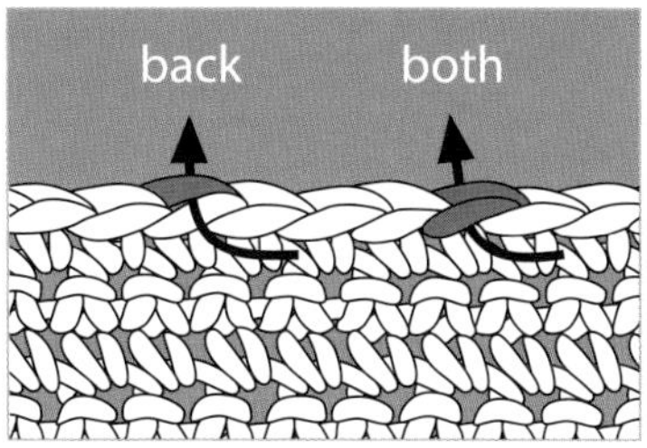

FREE LOOPS OF A CHAIN

When instructed to work in free loops of a chain, work in loop indicated by arrow ***(Fig. 2)***.

Fig. 2

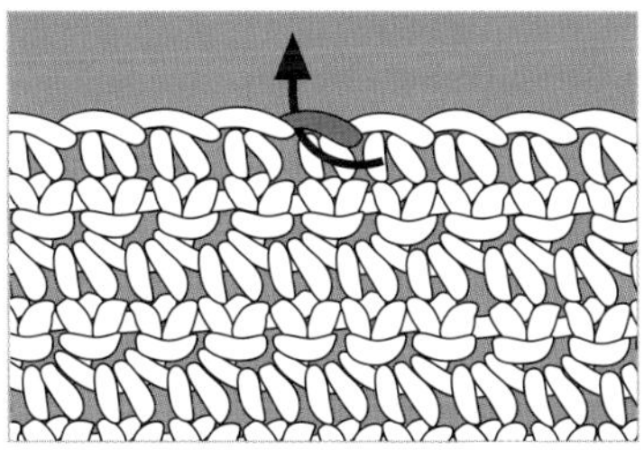

WHIPSTITCH

With **wrong** sides together, sew through both pieces once to secure the beginning of the seam, leaving an ample yarn end to weave in later. Insert the needle from **back** to **front** through **both** loops of each stitch ***(Fig. 3a)*** **or** through **inside** loops only of each stitch ***(Fig. 3b)*** on **both** pieces. Bring the needle around and insert it from **back** to **front** through the next loop(s) on both pieces.

Fig. 3a

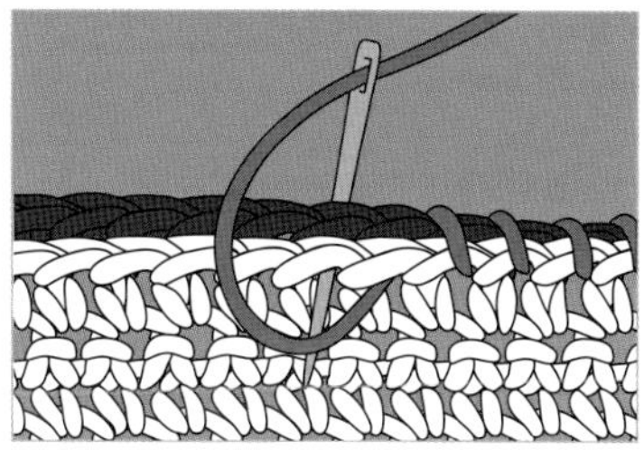

Fig. 3b

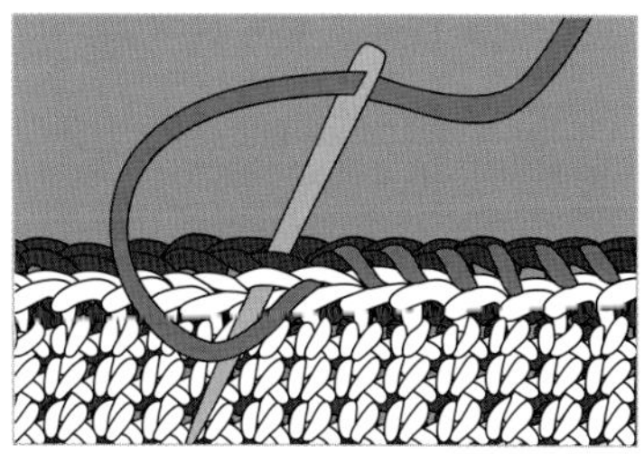

●○○○ BEGINNER	Projects for first-time crocheters using basic stitches. Minimal shaping.
●●○○ EASY	Projects using yarn with basic stitches, repetitive stitch patterns, simple color changes, and simple shaping and finishing.
●●●○ INTERMEDIATE	Projects using a variety of techniques, such as basic lace patterns or color patterns, mid-level shaping and finishing.
●●●● EXPERIENCED	Projects with intricate stitch patterns, techniques and dimension, such as non-repeating patterns, multi-color techniques, fine threads, small hooks, detailed shaping and refined finishing.

CROCHET HOOKS																	
U.S.	B-1	C-2	D-3	E-4	F-5	G-6	7	H-8	I-9	J-10	K-10½	L-11	M/N-13	N/P-15	P/Q	Q	S
Metric - mm	2.25	2.75	3.25	3.5	3.75	4	4.5	5	5.5	6	6.5	8	9	10	15	16	19

Meet Kristi Simpson

Inspired by her love of yarn, Kristi Simpson creates crochet and knit patterns with a fresh and modern touch. The mother of five became hooked on crochet after teaching herself so she could help her daughter make a scarf from a "learn to crochet" kit that was a gift.

"I loved it from the beginning," she says. "I was amazed that I could take a string of yarn and create something so useful and pretty! Needless to say, I never stopped!"

Other Leisure Arts books featuring Kristi's designs include Huggable Amigurumi (#7163), Messy Bun Hats Plus! (#7122), Color Block Baby Blankets (#7104), Urban Slouch Hats (#6796), Easy Essential Bags (#6795), Animal Baby Bibs (#6850), Animal Blankets (#6996), Sweet & Sporty Diaper Covers (#6719), Modern Baby Booties (#6914), and more to come soon. Visit kristisimpson.net or find her on Ravelry, Facebook, and Pinterest.

Yarn Information

Each project in this book was made with Bulky or Super Bulky Weight T-shirt Yarn. Any brand may be used. It is best to refer to the yardage/meters when determining how many ball or skeins to purchase. Remember, to arrive at the finished size, it is the GAUGE/TENSION that is important, not the brand of yarn.

For your convenience, listed below are the yarns used to create our photography models. Because yarn manufacturers make frequent changes in their product lines, you may sometimes find it necessary to use a substitute yarn or to search for the discontinued product at alternate suppliers (locally or online).

HEXAGON MOTIF RUG
Lion Brand® Fast-Track®
White - #100 Airstream White
Black - #153 Jet Black
Pink - #195 Pink Convertible

COASTER & PLACEMAT SET
Bernat® Maker Home Dec™
#11004 Green Pea
#11006 Steel Blue
#11009 Cream

OVAL RUG
Bernat® Maker Home Dec™
Grey - #11008 Clay
Variegated - #11017 Lilac Fence Varg

BASKET SET
Bernat® Maker Home Dec™
#11009 Cream
#11019 Pebble Beach Varg

TEXTURED PILLOW
Bernat® Maker Home Dec™
#11009 Cream

STRIPED BASKET
Lion Brand® Fast-Track®
Grey - #149 Chopper Grey
White - #100 Airstream White
Purple - #146 Purple Train

TOTE
Bernat® Maker Home Dec™
#11009 Cream
#11012 Black

LARGE POUF
Lion Brand® Fast-Track®
Blue - #108 Dune Buggy Denim
Grey - #149 Chopper Grey

DOILY RUG
Bernat® Maker Home Dec™
#11006 Steel Blue

THROW
Bernat® Maker Home Dec™
#11006 Steel Blue

We have made every effort to ensure that these instructions are accurate and complete. We cannot, however, be responsible for human error, typographical mistakes, or variations in individual work.

Production Team: Instructional/Technical Editor - Cathy Hardy; Editorial Writer - Susan Frantz Wiles; Senior Graphic Artist - Lora Puls; Graphic Artist - Kellie McAnulty; Photo Stylist - Lori Wenger; and Photographer - Jason Masters.

Made In U.S.A.